ISBN: 979869013770

But...

...I Just Can't Get Out Of Bed!

Bible study for young people
who are struggling to throw off
the duvet and start the day.

How to use this book

This book is divided into sections:

Prepare - is an opportunity to reflect on your starting point, either individually or in a group discussion.

Bible Study - time to dig deeper into God's word. You will need a Bible handy to complete this section.

Reflection - creative writing to lead you into prayer and reflection.

Going Deeper - offers ideas for personal prayer and reflection.

Ideas for Larger Youth Groups - suggests games, projects and ideas for youth leaders in a large group setting.

Ideas for All Age Worship - suggests ways in which young people could share their learning with God's people of all generations.

Introduction

Everybody craves the odd duvet-day, and tiredness in the morning is a normal part of teenage physiology. But sometimes that inability to throw off the covers and start the day has its roots in something more than just growing pains.

In this booklet you will find studies to help you dig deep, to think about what is keeping you under the covers, and to find out how an active prayer-life can become and healthy and life-giving start to day.

How to find a Bible Passage

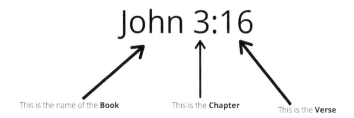

John 3:16

This is the name of the **Book**   This is the **Chapter**   This is the **Verse**

Go to the **Contents** page of your Bible and look up the name of the **book**. (Old Testament and New Testament books might be listed separately, or in alphabetical order instead of page order.)

Within each book, the larger numbers at the head of each section are the **chapter** numbers, and the smaller ones within the text are the **verse** numbers.

Prepare

What time does your alarm go off?

And what goes through your head when it does?

Which of these images best sums up your feelings about alarm clocks?

Do you think that there is anything in the Bible that will help you to feel better about starting the day?

Your Thoughts and Reflections.

Use this space to note down your responses to the 'prepare' questions, and any thoughts and feelings as you begin this study book.

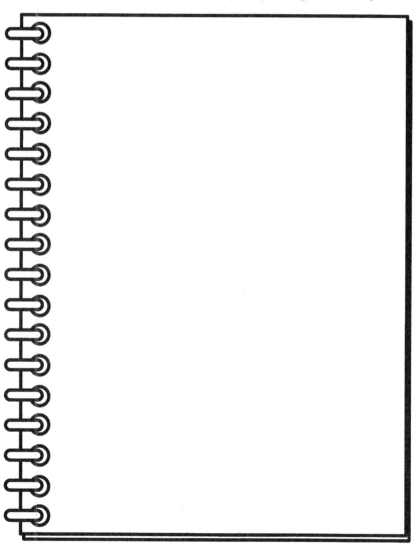

Bible Study 1

But...
...I just can't face the day!

What makes this day special?

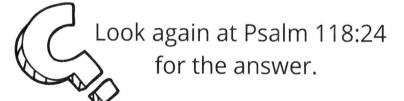

Psalm 118:1-29

Look again at Psalm 118:24 for the answer.

 The Psalms are ancient songs and poems that have been used in worship for centuries. The writers of the Psalms pour out their hearts with raw honesty - which sometimes leads to shocking results! (Turn to Psalm 137:9 to see what I mean, but only if you have a strong stomach!)

At times, this brutal honesty might make us want to squirm, but it also gives us the assurance that we can come before God with whatever we are feeling, whenever we are feeling it.

Sometimes, when we don't feel able to face the day (and particularly - other people), it is because we are feeling pretty low about ourselves. At its most severe, this feeling can be a symptom of anxiety or depression - mental health conditions which should be discussed with a doctor.

However, a mild case of morning blues now and then is also normal part of life, especially (but not exclusively) for young people. In Psalm 118 the writer knows there are enemies out there (see verses 6 and 7) and yet is able to celebrate the start of a new day (see verse 24) and march triumphantly into a world filled with friends and enemies alike. Let's find out where our psalmist finds that courage...

 What is the first verse of Psalm 118, and what is the last verse?

Does this beginning and ending give us any clues about what comes in the middle?

Have you ever felt like everyone was against you and there was no-one on your side? Our psalmist certainly did! In verses 10-13 the writer describes being encamped for battle, surrounded by enemies.

In verses 14-15, what does the psalmist do in order to summon up courage?

Your Notes

Some Bible translations describe those in the tent as singing, whilst others have them shouting for joy. Both are reasonable translations from the original Hebrew. Which do you prefer, and why?

The psalmist knows he is not perfect, but he still has hope. What is he hoping for in verses 17-18?

Do the words in verse 22 sound familiar? They pop up quite a few times in the Bible. Check out some of these occurrences:

- Matthew 21:42
- Mark 12:10
- Luke 20:17
- 1 Peter 2:4-7

A cornerstone is the first stone laid in any construction, often carved with a ceremonial inscription. You may have heard the word 'cornerstone' used as a metaphor for 'the most important thing.' What do you think the 'cornerstone' is in Christian thought? (Hint: Acts 4:11)

The psalmist has hope because of this cornerstone - but why? Verse 21 gives the answer, and so does Acts 4:12.

Your Notes

The psalmist begins and ends the Psalm by declaring that God's love endures forever. This means not only forwards in time, but backwards too!

Even though Jesus hadn't been born yet, the psalmist has a vision, a sense of hope, about the coming mercy of God - a mercy that will reach back in time, covering past mistakes.

Somehow, a memory of past mistakes can turn a simple duvet into a ten ton weight! We remember the argument we got into yesterday, or the bad result we got when we didn't study for a test last week - these memories make us feel bad, and before long we are saying to ourselves - 'I always mess up' or 'everyone is against me'.

Sometimes, it can feel like all our past errors and blunders are encamped around us, or buzzing around our heads, just like the psalmist's enemies.

But what did the psalmist do?

- The psalmist remembered the constant, relentless, unwavering love of God. (Verses 1 and 29)
- The psalmist remembered all the good things that God had done, and turned them into a song of praise. (Verses 5-13)
- The psalmist sang songs of praise in the tent, or perhaps even shouted for joy, in order to summon up the courage to go out and face those enemies. (Verses 14-16)
- The psalmist remembered that, although God takes sin seriously, he also saves us from sin's power. (Verses 17-23)

Most importantly, the psalmist reminds us to start every day afresh with that promise of mercy. (Verse 24)

In verse 27 we see that the psalmist now has the courage to dance joyfully in the morning light, - and so should we!

Your Notes

Reflection

But ...I Just Can't Get Out Of Bed!

Let me say, "Help me to start the day!"
when I feel all alone, with the whole world to fight;
when all I can think about are bad things I've done –
though brutal honesty makes me want to hide!

When I feel all alone, with the whole world to fight,
God is there, with any thought, anytime, any place!
Though brutal honesty makes me want to hide –
it is the cornerstone that clears the way ahead!

God is there, with any thought, anytime, any place –
His gifts of love, vision, and a fresh sense of hope.
It is the cornerstone that clears the way ahead –
a promise of mercy and a fresh start!

His gifts of love, vision, and a fresh sense of hope,
when all I can think about are bad things I've done.
A promise of mercy and a fresh start –
let me say, "help me to start the day"!

M. McKinnell

In Deep

Ideas for Responding in Prayer

Ready to dabble:
Quick and simple prayer ideas

Make a list of things that have gone well for you in recent days. Has anyone paid you a compliment? Did the bus come on time? Did you manage to dodge that rain shower? Is the room you are in right now warm and comfortable?

Write them all down, every little thing. Then recite them, just like the psalmist does (verse 17), starting each line with 'Thank you God...'

Going deeper:
Ideas to try if you have more time

Find a quiet place, and spend a bit of time looking at 1 Corinthians 13:4-7. Try writing the verses out, or saying them quietly to yourself, replacing the word 'love' each time it occurs with your own name.

Which one was hardest to write/say? Do you feel like you are not always as patient as you should be? Or perhaps not always kind?

Ask God to make THIS the day where you get a little better in one area or another. You could write out the word 'love' or another word from the passage (such as 'Patient') in bubble writing and colour it mindfully as you pray.

Space for Journalling

Diving right in:

Ideas for personal prayer and journalling

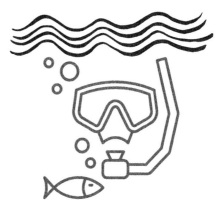

Why not take time this week to write down 3 things you are thankful for every day?

Keep these in a notebook or prayer journal to look back on when you are feeling low in a morning.

Create a Morning Ritual of Praising God

Step 1: Choose a motivational 'slogan' from the Bible, such as "This is the day that the LORD has made!" or "Sing a new song to the LORD!"

Write your slogan on a card or a sticky note and put it on top of your alarm clock/glasses/phone screen so that it is the first thing you see every morning.

Step 2: Take a big breath in, hold it for a count of 5, then say (or sing!) your slogan as you breathe out.

Step 3: Repeat step 2 until that duvet starts to feel a little less heavy!

Step 4: On another sticky note, write out Psalm 139:14. Stick this note to your mirror so that you see it every day, or set it as a recurring reminder on your phone.

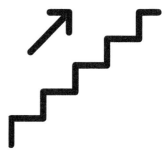

Space for Journalling

 # Games and Ideas for Groups

Put on the Armour of God

Divide the young people into two or more teams. Give each team an old newspaper and a roll of masking tape. Challenge them to look up Ephesians 6:14-18 and dress up one member of their team in the 'armour' described. Then take away the Bibles and have a quiz - what do all the bits of armour stand for? (i.e. Belt of **truth**, sword of **The Spirit.**)

If the young people wear school uniform, encourage them to re-write the passage as if their uniform was the armour. (i.e. Tie of... Shirt of...)

Worship Wall

Cover a large section of wall with lining paper or flip-chart paper, and encourage the young people to 'graffiti' the wall with things they want to thank God for, or to imagine they are the psalmist in Psalm 118 - what would he write?

Hey - I'm OK!

Many young people have an overly negative view of themselves, and think others see them the same way. Tape a sheet of paper to the back of each young person, and issue everyone with a pen. Set an allotted amount of time for everyone to go around the room and write anonymous compliments on other people's backs. (You may need to agree some ground rules, such as no 'back-handed' compliments and don't just focus on personal appearance.)

At the end of the time, allow everyone to read what has been written by others, and discuss how they feel about what people have said.

Ideas for
All Age Worship

Psalm 118 is a processional psalm, probably sung by the people as they entered their place of worship.
In verses 2-4, the different groups of worshippers are encouraged to lift their voices one-by-one.

The young people could write their own version of this call-and-response prayer to lead the wider congregation, coming up with their own categories, i.e.

All those who are young say:
His love endures forever!
All those who are wearing glasses say:
His love endures forever!
All those who have the letter 'E' in their name say:
His love endures forever!
All those sitting in the choir say:
His love endures forever!

It can also be very powerful, if you have enough space and enough young people, for them to process from the back of the worship space to the front, reciting the Psalm as they go. The young people may want to choose a symbol, such as a cross or a candle, to have at the front of their procession. They may also want to rewrite the Psalm in their own words.

Depending on space, the whole congregation could be invited to join the procession as it passes. It is good to 'prime' certain individuals in advance to do this, so that others are able to overcome shyness and inhibition about joining in..

Bible Study 2

But...
...My life feels pointless!

What does God do slowly?

Psalm 145:1-21

Look again at
Psalm 145:8
for the answer.

What is the meaning of life?

One of the Church's most famous sayings is this:

"What is the chief end of man*?"
"Man's chief end is to glorify God, and enjoy him forever."

*By 'man' they mean 'humanity' - male and female.

This phrase comes not from the Bible directly, but from an old teaching book called the Catechism. Even since the earliest days of Christianity, people have asked about the meaning of life.

Sometimes, if we're finding it hard to get up and start the day, it's because we don't have a feeling of purpose or direction to propel us out from under the covers. This is especially true when we are young, and we don't have responsibilities like work or parenthood which mean we simply *have* to get up! It's easy to think we're not important, and that a wasted day doesn't matter.

In Psalm 145 our psalmist, who claims to be King David himself, tells us what he thinks about the purpose of his life.

If you were the king of a great nation like David, what do you think you would say about the purpose of your life?

What do you think your duties would be every day?

Cow = Emergency colouring in.

Compare your thoughts on a king's daily duty with verses 1 and 2 of the Psalm. Is it the same, or different?

Your Notes

What about your own life? (Assuming you're not actually a king!) Do you have duties and responsibilities?

What activities give you a feeling of purpose?

What two things does David say "I will..." do, in verses 5 and 6?

Why do you think King David spends time on these activities? Look at verses 19 and 20 for some clues.

When and where do you (or could you) spend time on these activities in your own daily life?

Do you think these activities would give you a sense of purpose?

Look carefully through verses 14-20, and make a list of all the things God does.

The psalmist's list of God's good deeds in these verses is an example of meditating on God's wonderful works. We can almost imagine King David lying in his bed, reciting this list as he prepares to throw off the blankets and start the day.

What things would you put on your own list of God's good deeds?

What could you do to help you remember these things every day?

Your Notes

Glorifying God is all very well, but we all have personal desires and ambitions in life too.

Sometimes we worry that our personal ambitions are not going to match up with God's will. (What if God doesn't want me to become a rock star?)

 What do you think verses 16-19 tell us about how to bring our personal desires and ambitions to God?

Verse 20 contains some challenging words - 'The wicked God will destroy.'

This type of phrase is not unusual in the Psalms, and in other parts of the Old Testament, but it seems to fly in the face of Jesus teaching us to love our enemies!

They are difficult words, but they do come in context. In verse 9 the psalmist has already said that God is merciful to everything God has made, and verses 15 - 20 paint a picture of someone who is bowed down - life has dealt them a blow and they are waiting patiently for the justice of God.

Therefore we should probably read verse 20 as words of comfort to the oppressed, not as words of threat to the wicked! Justice is in God's hands; God will be merciful but God will also be fair.

Young people are forced to give a lot of attention to personal goals: exam results, career development, finding a life partner. But King David has achieved all that (and then some!)

David is at the top and can go no higher. Who better to ask: what is the meaning of life? Looking at Psalm 145 as a whole, how would you summarise his answer? How does King David's answer compare with the quote from the catechism at the start of this study?

Your Notes

The psalmist (either King David, or someone imagining what it might be like to be King David) is someone at the top of his game.

Under the rule of King David, the Kingdom of Israel became the biggest and strongest that it had ever been! From humble beginnings as a shepherd boy, David had reached the top of the pile and achieved all his life's ambitions. But this only revealed the brutal truth: when you're at the top, the only way is down.

If we're tempted to hit snooze, turn over and skive the day - it may because we don't feel a sense of purpose in our lives. After all, what is the point? Even if we get to the top, we'll only slide right back down again.

But in Psalm 145, King David show us that, even at the top, there's always something higher - and that something is the glory of God!

- Instead of looking down from the dizzying heights he has achieved, David looks up to God. (Verse 1)
- He sees that every day of his life is an opportunity to worship God, whose greatness is unfathomable. (Verses 2 - 3)
- He seizes every day as an opportunity to meditate on, and speak about God's greatness, and to compel others to do the same. (Verses 4 - 13)
- He brings his hopes, fears and ambitions to God, trusting that God will protect and provide. (Verses 14 - 20)

As a young person, you may have fewer duties and responsibilities than others around you - but Psalm 145 teaches us that you do have at least one duty: To glorify God and enjoy him forever.

Your Notes

 **Reflection**

But ...I Just Can't Get Out Of Bed!

The time is now, this minute, this day –
but stuck at a crossroads, my signpost unclear;
expectations from others cloud up the mind –
that voice in my head, "there's simply no point!"

Stuck at a crossroads, my signpost unclear –
God's plan seems at odds with my ambition once more;
that voice in my head, "there's simply no point" –
can I just put it off, for just one more day?

God's plan seems at odds with my ambition once more.
But focus on God seems always the best;
can I just put it off, for just one more day?
But I've to remember praising God never ends!

Focus on God seems always the best –
expectations from others cloud up the mind;
but I've to remember praising God never ends –
the time is now, this minute, this day.

M. McKinnell

In Deep

Ideas for Responding in Prayer

Ready to dabble:

Quick and simple prayer ideas

In the year 1253 AD, Bishop Richard of Chichester is thought to have written this famous prayer:

Day by day, Dear Lord, of thee three
things I pray:
To see thee more clearly,
To love thee more dearly,
To follow thee more nearly,
Day by day.

Bishop Richard became famous for his constant devotion to God and his unselfish and charitable way of living. Try praying his prayer and asking God to help you live a life of worship and service to others.

Going deeper:

Ideas to try if you have more time

Spend some time reflecting on Bishop Richard's prayer (above), either alone or in a group.

- Which aspect of it do you find the hardest?
- What does it mean to 'see' our invisible God?
- What does it mean to 'follow' our invisible God?

One place where we 'follow' people is on social media. Who do you choose to 'follow' on social media and why?

Space for Journalling

Diving right in:
Ideas for personal prayer and journalling

Take a page in your prayer journal to tell God (with honesty) where you see yourself in five years time, ten years time and fifty years time.

Read Psalm 145:18 again, then offer your ambitions prayerfully to God.

Read John 10:1-11. What does an 'abundant' or 'full' life mean to you?

In the Psalm, Kind David makes a number of 'I will...' statements. Try filling out the prayer of Bishop Richard by inserting you own 'I will...' statements after each line. Here is an example:

To see thee more clearly,
I will... *spend some time in nature today, admiring your creation.*
To love thee more dearly,
I will... *not skip my prayer time today, but spend some time focussed on you.*
To follow thee more nearly,
I will...*make an effort to show kindness to those around me today.*

At the end of the day, go back over what you have written. Did you live up to your 'I will...' statements?

Do you think making these commitments gave you a stronger sense of duty and purpose?

Space for Journalling

Games and Ideas for Groups

Follow the Leader

Sit the young people in a circle, and send one person out of the room to be the 'detective'. Select one young person in the circle as the 'leader'. The leader must then choose an action for the group to do - something like clapping, clicking, patting heads, tapping feet etc. The leader can change the action whenever they like, but they must try to avoid the detective catching them doing so. When the detective figures out who the leader is, the game is over and a new detective and leader can be chosen. Lead this into a discussion on how we can 'follow' God by imitating Christ.

From One Generation to the Next

We often moan about old Church buildings - enormous, impossible to heat and difficult to renovate! However, we should not forget the reason why these buildings are so ornate - they were built to last, and designed to inspire future generations with a sense of the majesty and glory of God. Type 'amazing Church buildings' or 'inspiring Church buildings' into a search engine, and take a look at some of the fantastic Churches that are declaring God's glory all around the world.

Challenge the young people to design their own Church building. You could do this by junk-modelling, using Lego/construction toys, or by using computer simulation games. What type of building do they think will inspire future generations with a sense of God's glory?

God Cares for All Things

Send the young people out into nature and challenge them to take a photo of something small and (seemingly) insignificant - such as an insect or a tiny flower - something that God cares for, even though we hardly notice it. Put the photos together in a slideshow or on a social media site under the same hashtag, and ask a young person to read Matthew 6:25-34 as you scroll prayerfully through the photos.

Ideas for All Age Worship

The 'God Cares for All Things' activity from the 'Games and Ideas for Groups' section could be adapted for All Age Worship, depending on the technology available in your worship space. If you have a screen, the young people could prepare a slideshow of pictures for the congregation and choose some prayerful music to accompany it, or read the Psalm out loud slowly as the pictures scroll through. If you don't have a screen, you could challenge the congregation to go out through the week and take some pictures of their own, uploading them to a social media site with a particular hashtag (please be aware of age restrictions on some social media sites), or emailing them in to be printed on a notice board/displayed on your Church website.

Psalm 145 highlights the duty of one generation telling another about God's goodness. Give each member of the congregation a slip of paper with the sentence starter, "I have known the goodness of God..." and ask them to write a line or two. It might be something as simple as when they have seen a spectacular sunset, or a personal story about a time in their life when God has helped them or answered their prayers. The slips could be kept anonymous if people prefer.

Display the responses somewhere, or have them read aloud (perhaps read a few at the start of each service over a number of weeks?) so that all generations can hear about the goodness of God.

Bible Study 3

But...
...Everybody hates me!

Who can come into
God's house?

Psalm 5:1-12

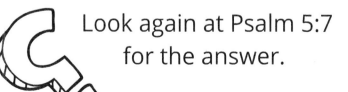

Look again at Psalm 5:7
for the answer.

Are you really that tired? Or are you just hiding from the world? After all, the world for young people can be a pretty harsh place.

Whether it's school bullies who hate you *just because*, or catty 'frenemies' who sell you out for a bit of social capital - there are times when it feels like no-one is on your side.

No wonder that sometimes we want to burrow under the covers and never come out! That's certainly how our psalmist (King David, or someone imagining what it was like to be him) was feeling in Psalm 5. He was lying on his bed, dreading the day to come, and we are given the chance to eavesdrop on his heartfelt prayer.

The last word of verse 1 is often translated as 'lament' or 'complaint' - but in Hebrew it is actually a word for groaning or even growling! The psalmist is asking God to pay attention, not only to his words, but also to the dark, uncomfortable feeling that he has inside.

Can you identify with the psalmist here? Do you sometimes feel things that are difficult to express to God, or to other people, using words?

In verses 4-6 the psalmist sets out a list of his enemies' crimes. What does he accuse them of?

How does the psalmist think God feels about his enemies?

Jesus teaches us to love our enemies and pray for them, yet here is the psalmist saying God hates them! The Psalms are full of this kind of raw, human emotion. Of course, the truth is that while God takes sin seriously, God is also more full of mercy than we can ever imagine.

The psalmist's words might seem un-Christian, but they are a reminder that we can be honest with God in prayer. We don't have to 'clean up' our thoughts and feelings before we come to God. God came to us in Jesus - God knows what it is to be human!

Your Notes

In verse 10 the psalmist prays that his enemies will bring about their own downfall.

There is real wisdom here: catty and vicious people become known as such, and in the long term it does them no favours.

In verse 3 the psalmist has set out a two stage plan to help him cope in the meantime. What are the two things that he will do?

When you are lying in bed feeling unable to get up, how can you follow the psalmist's example?

Verse 7 speaks about God's house or temple. In the days of the psalmists, it was common to speak about the temple as if it was a house where God 'lived'. However, it s clear that this was just a way of speaking, rather than something that everybody believed, because the Old Testament is full of people praying to God everywhere and anywhere!

Even so, what's a good place for you to go if you really want to focus on prayer?

Some Church buildings are open through the day, and some public spaces offer a multi-faith prayer space. Have you ever used one of these spaces?

Cruel words are often described in the Old Testament as being like 'arrows' (Psalm 64:3) or like 'sharp swords' (Psalm 57:4) - and no wonder! When someone speaks cruelly to or about us, it can give rise to actual physical pain.

Have you ever felt that stabbing sensation? No doubt this is how the psalmist was feeling. But what does he describe in verses 11 and 12? How does this compare with the opening lines of the Psalm?

Your Notes

The psalmist feels like a victim. People are telling lies and speaking evil of him, and he is so depressed that he lies groaning, (or even growling!) in his bed. (Verse 1)

It hurts when we feel like there are people who take delight in speaking badly of us. It might be school bullies, online trolls, or sometimes even 'friends' whose brand of friendship we find we can do better without!

Their words are like sharp arrows or swords. Problem is, the bedcovers offer lousy protection against these vicious spears.

In Psalm 5, we get to eavesdrop on King David as he pours out heart and soul in honest prayer and braces himself to face the day.

- He trusts that God hears his prayer, spoken and unspoken. (Verses 1-3)
- He clings to the promise that God is not indifferent to sin. (Verses 4-6)
- He resolves to go to the temple, or a place of prayer, where he can focus his attention on God and wait for spiritual guidance. (Verses 7-8)
- He reminds himself that deceitful and cruel people are often the authors of their own downfall. (Verses 9-10)
- He places himself behind the 'shield' of his faith, and praises God as he waits for better times. (Verses 11-12)

The psalmist knows that the bedcovers won't protect him from anything - what he needs is the **shield** of faith (see Ephesians 6:16). It won't stop his enemies from making their attacks, but it will make him able to withstand them. So much so, that instead of growling on his bed, the psalmist finds the courage to rise and shine, singing songs of joy!

Your Notes

 **Reflection**

But ...I Just Can't Get Out Of Bed!

What courage to rise and shine from the dark,
when it feels no-one is by your side;
pierced by the swords and arrows of harsh words –
our shield of faith defends us always.

When it feels no-one is by your side –
only friends whose love we do better without;
yet our shield of faith defends us always –
as cruel words and deeds cause them to fall.

Friends whose love we do better without –
they too learn the world's a harsh place,
as their cruel words and deeds cause them to fall –
so love friend and foe as God teaches us to!

They too learn the world's a harsh place –
pierced by the swords and arrows of harsh words;
so love friend and foe as God teaches us to –
what courage to rise and shine from the dark!

M. McKinnell

In Deep

Ideas for Responding in Prayer

Ready to dabble:
Quick and simple prayer ideas

Wrap your arms around yourself as if you are giving yourself a hug! *Ahhh!*

Now recite the following prayer, based on verses 7-8 of the Psalm. Try saying the prayer slowly, out loud, and repeating it a few times over.

Jesus I give you my loneliness...
May your company be all I need.
Jesus I give you my fear...
May your majesty be the only thing that makes me tremble.
Jesus I give you this day...
Make the way of holiness straight before me.

Going deeper:
Ideas to try if you have more time

If you type 'heraldry symbols and meanings' into a search engine, you will find several websites which tell you about the symbols used on shields. An **anchor**, for example, stands for hope and salvation, while an **ant** stands for wisdom.

Think about what you are asking God for this day. Is it strength, or courage? Look up the heraldry symbols for these things, and design a shield for yourself, praying mindfully as you draw and colour.

Space for Journalling

Diving right in:

Ideas for personal prayer and journalling

Below you will find part of 'The Prayer of St Francis'.

This prayer might not have been written by St Francis himself, but no matter who wrote it, it is a phenomenal piece of text, packed with wisdom.

Read the prayer slowly, with a highlighter or a pencil in hand. Think of a situation in your own life where there is 'hatred' - and when you have thought of one, highlight or underline the word 'hatred'. Now think of a way that you might bring 'love' to that situation, and when you have thought of something (remembering that sometimes the 'only' thing we can do is pray), highlight or underline the word 'love'.

Keep working through the prayer until you have done this with all the keywords. (If you get really stuck on one, don't worry, just skip it and go to the next.)

The Prayer of St Francis (Excerpt)
Lord, make me an instrument of your peace.
Where there is hatred, let me bring love.
Where there is offence, let me bring pardon.
Where there is discord, let me bring union.
Where there is error, let me bring truth.
Where there is doubt, let me bring faith.
Where there is despair, let me bring hope.
Where there is darkness, let me bring your light.
Where there is sadness, let me bring joy.

This is only an excerpt - you may want to type 'Prayer of St Francis' into a search engine and read the remainder of the prayer.

Space for Journalling

Games and Ideas for Groups

'Tails'

Give each young person a 30cm length of wool or string. This is their 'tail' and they must tuck it lightly into the back of their clothes, leaving at least 20cm dangling like a tail. Encourage the young people to spread out in a large open space, and when you shout 'go' they have to try and capture other people's tails without losing their own! Once a player loses their tail they are out, but they should keep hold of any tails that they have captured. The game ends when all but one has lost their tail, but the winner is the person who has captured the most tails. Afterwards, talk about what it feels like to play this game - what's it like to always have to 'watch your back'?

All Under One Banner

The heraldry activity in 'going deeper' is suggested for personal prayer, but the true purpose of decorated shields was to help soldiers to quickly identify their comrades on the battlefield.

Choosing symbols which are meaningful, ask the young people to design a shield for your youth group or church family - perhaps using graphic design software or making a large display version out of cardboard.

Prayer of St Francis Relay Race

Print out two copies of the prayer of St Francis, cutting each line in half. At one end of the room place the "Where there is..." statements: this is the team 'base'. At the other end place the "Let me bring..." statements, jumbled up. Divide the young people into two teams. Each team must complete the prayer at their 'base' by sending a runner to select the correct "Let me bring..." statement. Only one runner can be out of the base at a time. The winning team is the first to complete the prayer.

Ideas for All Age Worship

The **'Prayer of St Francis'** can easily be incorporated into All Age Worship, as it has been set to music many times. To engage younger children it may be helpful to devise some actions, or learn the Makaton, to go along with the prayer as it is spoken or sung.

It can also be prayed in a call-and-response way:

Lord, make me an instrument of your peace.
Where there is hatred, **let me bring love.**
Where there is offence, **let me bring pardon.**
...
Or, if you have young readers, put the repeated bits (which are easier to read) in bold for all to say:

Lord, make me an instrument of your peace.
Where there is hatred**, let me bring** love**.**
Where there is offence**, let me bring** pardon**.**

...

If you have completed the heraldry activity, this may be something that the young people enjoy sharing with the wider congregation.

Bible Study 4

But...
...I'm just too lazy to get up!

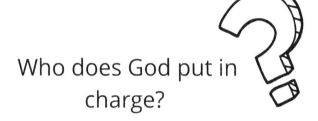

Who does God put in charge?

Matthew 25:14-30

Look again at Matthew 25:21 for the answer.

OK, we've tried being nice, but you're still lying in bed. Sorry guys, but it's time for a kick in the pants!

Several times in this study booklet we've said that God takes sin seriously. Often we think of sin as things we have said or things we have done that are wrong.

However, there is also another category of sin, which are sometimes called 'sins of omission'. This is where there are things we have **not** said or things we have **not** done, even though we should have.

Sins of omission are easy to make - not giving to charity, not remembering to pray for someone when we said we would. Right there on the list is not getting out of bed and not seizing every day as an opportunity to serve God...

Pay attention to the context of the parable in Matthew 25:14-30. The rest of chapter 25 is a continuation of Jesus speaking, but what are the events that happen in chapter 26?

Who do you think the man is in verse 14? Could it be Jesus? If so, what is the journey he is speaking about?

What does your Bible say the man entrusted to his servants? Some translations will say 'bags of gold', others use the word 'talents'.

In modern English, the word 'talent' has come to mean 'something you are good at' - but this wasn't always what that word meant. In the time of Jesus a 'talent' was a sum of money - about twenty years worth of wages for the average worker.

Your Notes

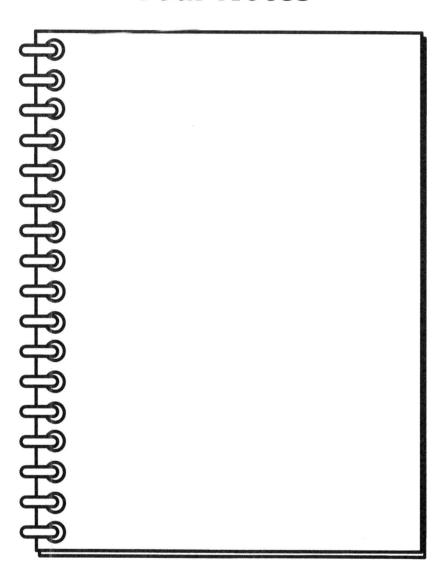

In the ancient world, money was measured by weight, so a 'talent' referred to the distance that the scales were leaning. Thus, the earliest meaning of the word 'talent' (when not referring to money) was 'a leaning or inclination' towards something.

As young people it can sometimes feel like we don't have any 'talents' - since we are still learning and perfecting our skills.

But what if we take that older meaning of the word?

What kind of activities do you feel you have a 'leaning or inclination' towards?

What will happen to your 'talents' if you stay lying in bed every morning, and never find the motivation to use or develop them?

Whilst we can never 'earn' our salvation by working for it, nevertheless the Bible makes it clear that God has work for us to do!

Look up some of the following verses. What things do they teach us about 'work'?

- Colossians 3:23
- Exodus 20:9
- Ephesians 3:20
- Galatians 6:3-5
- Philippians 2:12
- 1 Timothy 5:25

Your Notes

God gives us the ability to do many things to serve. Some people are gifted for very 'visible' ministries in the Church, such as teaching or providing music, but just as important, if not more important, are those who serve outside the Church - showing God's love and kindness in the community, often in very quiet ways.

In what ways could your 'talents' be used to serve the Church or the community, either now or in the future?

When the man questions the servant who buried his talent, what reason does the servant give for his actions? (Verse 25)

Does the Master accept this excuse? (Verse 26)

What two things does he accuse the servant of being? Does this seem a bit harsh?

Fear and laziness sound like two different things, but they are not always unrelated. **Fear** is an emotion and **laziness** is a behaviour. Our behaviours are usually driven by our emotions - so if we have a persistent problem with laziness, it might be worth looking in the mirror and saying, "Am I actually afraid of something?"

What does the Master say his servant should have done instead of burying his talent? (Verse 27)

Your Notes

Jesus knew the final part of his journey had come. Soon He would leave his disciples to carry on His work. They needed to understand how important this work was!

When Jesus first left them, it seemed like the disciples would be a bit like that servant who hid his talent in the ground: they locked themselves in the upper room, hiding from the crowds. But then the Spirit of God came upon them (Acts 2) and suddenly the disciples had talents they could never even have dreamed of!

In Matthew 25, the servant with only one talent let his fear lead him into laziness - a sin of omission. The Master says that, if he was too afraid of failure to use his talent, then he should have taken his talent to the bankers - in other words, he should have got some help.

As we said at the start of study 1 - a mild case of morning blues now and then, a bit of tiredness or a reluctance to throw off the duvet, is a pretty normal part of being young. Hopefully these Bible studies, and the suggestions for personal prayer, have helped you to rethink what goes in that thought bubble when your alarm clock goes off. (See the **prepare** page.)

However, if you are persistently feeling unable to get out of bed, persistently feeling like there is no point to your life, persistently feeling that everybody hates you, or persistently feeling that you have nothing to give, then it may be time to call the bankers for some help.

The 'bankers' in this case are the adults or elder Christians around you - people who God has put in your life to nurture your health and wellbeing. The right 'bankers' will listen to your struggles, offer prayer and spiritual wisdom, and help you to access professional counselling if needed.

After all, getting up in the morning is not just about keeping parents, teachers or employers happy - it is no more and no less than an act of obedience and service to God. When we truly understand that, we can truly understand the importance of throwing off that duvet!

Your Notes

Reflection

But ...I Just Can't Get Out Of Bed!

In every thought, every word, and every deed,
the work is important, serving God's Kingdom;
I hear you cry, "that job's beyond me",
but there's nowhere to run, and nowhere to hide!

This work is important, serving God's Kingdom –
just remember one thing - you're not alone;
there's nowhere to run, nowhere to hide –
remember to ask, the help will come!

Just remember one thing - you're not alone –
the Spirit will provide the talents and the works;
remember to ask, the help will come –
all God's workers are valued and loved!

The Spirit will provide the talents and the works –
I hear you cry, "that job's beyond me";
but all God's workers are valued and loved,
in every thought, every word, and every deed!

M. McKinnell

In Deep

Ideas for Responding in Prayer

Ready to dabble:
Quick and simple prayer ideas

Look again at the list you have made of your own 'talents'. Some will be skills and gifts you already have, and some will be leanings or inclinations - things you would like to get better at.

Using a collection plate borrowed from Church, or any large plate, write each talent slowly and prayerfully onto a slip of paper, then place each one onto the plate.

Say the following prayer as you do so: **Master, I give you this talent because I want to serve you.**

Going deeper:
Ideas to try if you have more time

A little trick for getting out of bed in the morning is to visualise the day ahead. Many adults do this unthinkingly, ("I must get up and feed the cat, then I want some coffee, then I must iron that shirt for work...") but it works for young people too.

Mentally walking through your day helps your brain move from sleep mode to awake mode. If you don't believe me - try it! And do you know what makes it even more effective? Mentally walking though your day with Jesus by your side. Imagine He's with you as you visualise munching your cereal, imagine He's with you as you visualise packing your bag. (NB: You might want to imagine He's politely looking the other way while you're taking your shower!)

Space for Journalling

Diving right in:
Ideas for personal prayer and journalling

The topics addressed in this book were selected using a tool called 'The Wheel of Emotion'. The original wheel was designed by a psychologist called Robert Plutchik, and there are now many versions in use, which you can find easily by typing 'Wheel of Emotion' into a search engine.

Feelings like 'apathetic' or 'weary' - the things which stop us getting out of bed - tend to relate to the 'unpleasant emotions' segments of the wheel, whereas 'energised' and 'courageous' relate to the 'pleasant' emotions. This is why these studies have addressed those central feelings such as fear, anger and sadness.

Looking at what you wrote in the thought bubble in the **prepare** section of this booklet, or reflecting on the feeling that you think is keeping you under the duvet in a morning, see if you can find your feeling somewhere on the Wheel of Emotion (Choose any version of the wheel that you find easy to navigate).

Which central segment(s) of the wheel do your feelings relate to? Have you ever taken your feelings honestly to God?

Turn to Psalm 139 in your Bible. Read the whole Psalm slowly, allowing the words to wash over you, and pausing wherever you want to. You may want to write out any significant verses or phrases in your prayer journal. Notice how, in verses 19-22, the psalmist does not hide his unpleasant feelings from God!

Now focus specifically on verses 23 and 24, asking God to show you what lies at the heart of everything you are feeling.

Space for Journalling

 # Games and Ideas for groups

The Carrot or the Stick

This is a game of calling someone's bluff. Take two identical boxes, place a carrot inside one box and a stick inside the other. Choose two players. Player one can look inside their box, but must not say what is in there. Player two cannot look inside their box, but must decide whether they want to keep their box or switch it with player one. They can ask player one questions, and player one has to answer them but is not required to tell the truth. Young people looking on should be encouraged to voice their opinions on whether player two should stick or switch! After an allotted time period (2 minutes is usually about right) player two must decide. Then comes the big reveal! Whoever has the carrot is the winner! Lead in to a discussion on fear of failure and/or what it is like to make decisions under pressure.

What Stops Us Using Our Talents?

Ask the young people to write on small circles of card (representing the coins in the parable) what they think their talents are. Encourage them to think beyond 'skills' such as music or sport and include 'attributes' such as being kind or generous. The talents should be placed in the bottom of a bucket or tray. Then, bring in some play sand or other suitable material such as shredded paper. The young people must name things that stop them using their talents (i.e. 'Fear of failure', 'Opinions of others') and, as they identify each one, they can take a handful of sand and 'bury' the talents. Later in the session you may want to ask them to un-bury the talents during a time of prayer.

Who's STILL in Bed?

A silly game to break the ice or finish off a session on a high note. Blindfold one person in the group and 'hide' a second one under a thick duvet. The blindfolded person must try to guess who is under the duvet by 'feeling' (yes, this game is HIGHLY inappropriate!) and listening for any squeaks or giggles. (No, there is no spiritual merit to this game whatsoever!)

Ideas for All Age Worship

The **'What Stops Us Using Our Talents?'** activity can be adapted for All Age Worship. Before the service, write out a number of attributes such as 'Generosity' 'Wisdom' 'Patience' 'Kindness' (1 Corinthians 13 and Galatians 5 can be consulted for additional ideas) on circles of card and 'bury' them in a tray of sand. At an appropriate point in the service, invite people to come and 'dig up' a talent, taking it away with them for prayerful reflection.

Another idea which can be adapted is taken from the 'Ready to Dabble' section above - give out blank circles of card and ask the congregation to write down one 'talent' which they think they can offer to God. You may want to highlight that a 'talent' can be a leaning or an inclination as well as a skill they already posses. Send round a collection plate to gather in the talents, and offer them to God using an offertory prayer or whatever feels natural for your congregation's style of worship.

One thing that all ages are really good at is excuses! Collect a number of shoe boxes (if you ask a local shoe shop they will gladly give you heaps!) or similar sized boxes (cereal boxes sort of work too). Ask everyone in the congregation to think of an excuse that they have made, or that someone might make, for not serving God (i.e. I'm too busy/tired/shy/afraid...) and write it on the box with a marker pen. (If they want to be more coy, they could write it on a slip of paper and put it inside the box.) Then use the boxes to build a great big wall between the congregation and the Altar or Table, or to obscure a significant feature in your worship space such as a cross.
Conduct the rest of the service with that ugly wall getting properly in the way. Then, at the end, or at an appropriate point, knock it down and have some volunteers clear all the rubbish excuses away!

About the Authors

H. C. Dill

Henna is a freelance writer and Christian youth worker. She lives in Aberdeenshire, Scotland with her husband and two children. Dill holds both a First Class Honours Degree and a Masters-by-Research in Theology from the University of Aberdeen. She has many years of experience in children and youth ministry, working with groups of all shapes and sizes, across different denominations.

To contact H. C. Dill, and to be kept up-to-date on future publications in this series, please visit the author's social media pages on Facebook (H.C.DillWrite) or Instagram (@h.c.dill.write).

M. McKinnell

Mary has an interest in Ignatian Spirituality, and much of her writing comes out of using spiritual practices from this tradition. She draws on scripture and on a wide variety of personal and church related experiences for inspiration.

An active Christian, with many years' experience working for the church as a communications mission officer, Mary enjoys helping others to communicate Christ's love to the local community. She is also a trained spiritual director and enjoys this ministry, listening to others and supporting them in their relationship with God.

Mary is available to lead worship services, reflective days and residential retreats to help people of all ages to spend time with God. You can view more of Mary's work or contact her via her blog: searchingforunderstanding.com

Printed in Great Britain
by Amazon